The
Ukrainian Christmas Cookbook

Marit Peters

© Copyright 2022 Marit Peters
All Rights Reserved

Contents

Introduction

Christmas is a popular period in Ukraine. Traditionally Christmas Day in Ukraine is on the 7 January as the Eastern Christian churches in Ukraine, such as the Orthodox church, use the Julian Calendar. The Western Christian Christmas Day 25 December is also a national holiday in the Ukraine.

Ukraine has a number of Christmas traditions that are familiar to other countries who celebrate Christmas. These include Christmas carols, Christmas markets, decorations, Christmas trees and other festive customs. Food naturally plays a key part. Christmas dinner on Christmas Eve has many typically Ukrainian dishes and traditionally does not contain meat, eggs or milk.

There are also many unique Ukrainian Christmas customs reflecting old beliefs and superstitions in the country. These all create a wonderful and unique festive period in Ukraine.

Sample the essence of Christmas in Ukraine with this book – The Ukrainian Christmas Cookbook.

Varenyky

Ingredients

dough

720g/6 cups of flour
3 tablespoons of butter
240ml/1 cup of sour cream
salt
180ml/2 thirds of a cup of water

filling

7 chopped potatoes
3 chopped onions
butter
120g/1 cup of grated cheese
salt
pepper

Mix the flour with some salt in a bowl. Add the sour cream and butter and mix adding water to make a dough. Place the dough in a bowl greased with oil for 40 minutes.

For the filling, put the potatoes on a pan. Cover with water. Bring to the boil. Cook for 12 minutes - until cooked. Drain the potatoes.

Put the onion in a pan with some butter and cook for 7 minutes. Mix the potato and onions in a bowl with some salt and pepper. Mix in the cheese.

Roll out the dough and cut into small circles. Put some filling on one side of a circle shape. Fold over and seal.

Put the dumplings in boiling water and cook for 5 minutes.

Borscht

Ingredients

500g/1.1 lb of chopped tomatoes
2 peeled and grated beetroot
1 peeled and diced beetroot
2 grated carrots
1 chopped potato
130g/4.5 oz of chopped celery
130g/4.5 oz of diced onions
130g/4. 5 oz of chopped cabbage
3 cloves of chopped garlic
butter
2 litres/9 cups of water
chopped fresh dill
sour cream
salt
pepper

Cook the onion, cabbage and celery in some butter in a pan for 8 minutes. Add the tomatoes, garlic and water. Bring to the boil add the beetroot, potato and carrot and cook on a low heat for 20 minutes.

Remove from the heat and add some salt and pepper and dill. Add some sour cream before serving.

Potato Pancakes

Ingredients

3 grated potatoes
2 beaten eggs
half a grated onion
3 tablespoons of flour
110g/half a cup of cottage cheese
salt
pepper

Mix the ingredients in a bowl. Heat some oil in a pan. Cook on a medium heat for 5 minutes on each side.

Cucumber Salad

Ingredients

6 peeled and sliced tomatoes
5 chopped spring onions/scallions
2 tablespoons of wine vinegar
1 tablespoon of sugar
oil
1 sliced cucumber
chopped parsley
salt
pepper

Put a layer of tomatoes on a plate. Add the onions.

Mix the sugar, vinegar and some salt and pepper. Mix with the oil then pour over the tomatoes.

Sprinkle the cucumbers with some salt. Later the cucumber on the tomatoes. Add some parsley. Place in the refrigerator for 5 hours.

Mashed Beans

Ingredients

360g/2 cups of haricot/white beans
1 chopped onion
2 cloves of garlic
oil
salt
pepper

Put the bean in some water and leave for 10 hours. Drain the beans. Place the beans in a pan and cover with water. Cook on a low heat for 3 hours. Drain the beans and mash them.

Cook the onion on a pan with some oil for 8 minutes. Add the garlic and cook for 2 minutes. Add some salt and pepper. Add to the mashed beans.

Lemon and Beetroot Soup

Ingredients

1.2 kg/2.6 lb of beetroot
2.5 litres/10 cups of vegetable stock
1 sliced lemon
3 egg whites
shells from 3 eggs
60ml/2.2 fl oz of lemon juice
salt
pepper

Wash the beetroot. Put in pan of salted water, cover, then boil for 40 minutes - until cooked.

Peel and dice the beetroot.

Put the stock, lemon slices and beetroot in a pan. Boil, cover, then cook on a low hat for 35 minutes. Strain the liquid into a bowl.

Put the liquid back in the pan and add the egg shells and whites. Bring to the boil and whisk. Cook on a low heat for 5 minutes.

Strain the liquid into another bowl. Heat the liquid in another pan for 5 minutes. Add the lemon juice and some salt and pepper.

Mushroom Soup

Ingredients

10 oz/280g of chopped mushrooms - for example
porcini/cep/penny bun
2 chopped potatoes
1 chopped onion
1 chopped carrot
4 chopped cloves of garlic
1.2 litres/5 cups of vegetable stock/broth
240ml/1 cup of milk
1 tablespoon of thyme
parsley
oil
salt
pepper

Put the carrot and onion in some oil in a pan and cook for 7 minutes.

Add the mushrooms and some more oil and cook for another 70 minutes. Put the vegetables in a bowl. Reserve some of the mushrooms to garnish the soup.

In the same pan put in the garlic and cook for 1 minute. Add the stock and boil. Add the potatoes then cook on a low heat for 12 minutes.

Add the vegetables back to the pan. Add the thyme and some salt and pepper. Cook on a medium heat for 7 minutes. Add the milk and cook for 5 minutes.

Blend the soup. Add some more salt and pepper. Garnish with mushrooms and parsley.

Crepes with Cheese

Ingredients

4 eggs
240ml/1 cup of milk
7 tablespoons of water
120g/1 cup of flour
2 egg yolks
450g/2 cups of cottage cheese
1 tablespoon of sour cream
chopped fresh dill
butter
salt

Beat the 4 eggs for 5 minutes. Add the flour, milk, water and some salt. Mix for 5 minutes to make a smooth batter.

Put some butter in a pan and heat. Pour some batter in the pan, spread it out, then cook the crepes for 1 minutes on each side.

For the filling mix the egg yolks, dill, sour cream and some salt.

Put the filling on the crepes and roll them up. Put the rolled up crepes in a baking dish. Put some butter on top then back in a preheated oven at 176C/350F for 22 minutes.

Ukraine Christmas Facts

In 2017 December 25th became an official holiday in the Ukraine. This is the Christmas Day of those Western Christian religions which follow the Gregorian calendar

The traditional Ukrainian Christmas according to Eastern Christian religions that follow the Julian calendar starts on January 6th - Christmas Eve - and ends on 19th January which is the date of Epiphany.

Christmas Eve is called Sviatvechir which means Holy Day in Ukraine.

One big traditional Ukrainian Christmas dish is Kutia. Kutia is a sweet grain pudding. It is the first dish served at Christmas Eve dinner.

Christmas Eve dinner begins after children spot the first star in the eastern sky.

Carol singers are popular in Ukraine during Christmas. It is thought that the more carol singers come to a person's home, the more luck and wealth they will have in the following year.

Potato Wedges

Ingredients

potatoes unpeeled and cut into wedges
dill
sunflower oil
sea salt

Put the potato wedges in a pan of boiling water. Cook for 8
minutes.

Coat the potato wedges in sunflower, some salt and dill.
Spread over a baking tray. cook in a preheated oven at
200C/392F for 35 minutes.

Stuffed Cabbage Roll

Ingredients

150g/5.3 oz of half cooked rice
1 grated carrot
1 chopped onion
leaves from 1 cabbage
2 garlic cloves
chopped parsley
550g/1.2 lb of minced/ground pork
3 chopped tomatoes
sour cream
black pepper
salt

Put the cabbage in a pan of salted boiling water. Cook for 3 minutes. Drain and put the cabbage leaves on a plate.

Put the onion and carrot in a pan with some oil and cook for 7 minutes.

Mix the rice, pork, tomatoes, garlic and some parsley together with some salt and pepper.

Put some of the filling in each cabbage leave and make enclosed cabbage rolls. Put the cabbage rolls in a pan. Spread the onion and carrot on top. Cover with boiled water. Cook on a low heat in the oven for 25 minutes. Add sour cream then cook for 35 minutes - until cooked.

Mushrooms in Tomato Sauce

Ingredients

300g/10.5 oz of chopped mushrooms
4 chopped tomatoes
2 chopped onion
260ml/9.1 fl oz of sour cream
60g/2.11 oz of butter
chopped fresh dill
salt
oil

Fry the onions in some oil for 7 minutes.

Add the mushrooms and cook for 6 minutes.

Add the sour cream and tomatoes. Cook on a low heat for 10 minutes.

Sprinkle some chopped fresh dill on top.

Pickled Watermelon

Ingredients

280g/10 oz of chopped water melon
500ml/2 cups of apple cider vinegar
100g/half a cup of sugar
3 tablespoons of lemon juice

Put the sugar, lemon juice and vinegar in a pan. Boil.

Put the watermelon into jars. Pour the hot liquid into the jars. Seal, then place in the refrigerator.

Borscht

Cabbage Rolls

Chicken in Jelly

Olivier Salad

Olivier Salad

Ingredients

6 diced gherkins
2 diced boiled potatoes
3 diced boiled carrots
5 diced boiled eggs
half a diced onion
396g/14 oz of diced ham
283g/10 oz tinned green peas
110g/half a cup of mayonnaise
salt
pepper
dill

Mix the ingredients in a bowl apart from the salt, pepper and dill. Add a little salt and pepper and some dill and mix.

Mushroom Dumplings

Ingredients

200g/7 oz of chopped mushrooms
60g/2.11 oz of chopped onion
60g/2. 11 oz of chopped carrot
400g/14 oz of flour
200ml/6.7 fl oz of water
oil
salt

Put the mushrooms, carrot and onion in a pan with some oil.
Cook for 10 minutes.

For the dough, mix the flour, water and some oil and salt to
make a dough. Leave for 30 minutes. Roll out the dough, then
make small circle shapes. Put some filling on the dough pieces
and enclose.

Bring a pan of water to the boil. Put the dumplings in and cook
for 5 minutes on a low temperature.

Ham Soup

Ingredients

1 baked ham
600g/1.3 lb of sauerkraut
1 onion
1 carrot
6 peppercorns
chopped parsley
200g/7 oz of corn grits
salt
pepper

Put the ham in a pan with 3 litres /12 and a half cups of water. Put the onion, carrot and peppercorns in the pan. Cook on a low heat for 35 minutes.

Strain the liquid. Put the liquid in another pan with the sauerkraut. Cook on a low heat for 15 minutes.

Chop the ham and add to the pan with the grits. Cook on a low heat for 15 minutes. Add some salt and pepper and parsley.

Carrot Patties

Ingredients

900g/2 lb of grated carrot
180g/6.2 oz of cottage cheese
3 tablespoons of semolina
2 tablespoons of sugar
2 eggs
120ml/half a cup of milk
salt
breadcrumbs

Put the carrot in a pan with the milk. Cook on a medium heat for 8 minutes - until the carrot is cooked.

Add the semolina, sugar and some salt to the pan. Cook on a medium heat for 10 minutes. Add the eggs and stir. Add the cottage cheese and mix.

Form the mix into patties. coat in breadcrumbs then fry in butter or oil for 6 minutes on each side - until crisp.

Ukraine Christmas Facts

On Christmas Eve dinner is a traditional twelve dish Christmas Eve supper. This is to commemorate Jesus' twelve disciples.

No meat, eggs or milk are allowed to be included in the dishes. Even though there are no meat ingredients fish is allowed and plays a big role in the supper. Grains and mushrooms are also common ingredients.

Ukrainians believe that their ancestors spend time with them during Christmas. The house is decorated with a wheat sheath called didukh with symbolises the spirits of ancestors.

On Christmas Day - January 7th - many Ukrainians go to church and then visit families and friends. Unlike Christmas Eve any type of food including meat is allowed to be eaten.

During Christmas dinner in Ukraine, hay is spread under the dinging table to remind everyone that Jesus was born in a manger.

Mushroom Gravy

Ingredients

450g/1 lb of dried porcini mushrooms
450g/1 lb of sliced mushrooms
1 chopped onion
1 chopped clove of garlic
oil
240ml/1 cup of sour cream
4 tablespoons of flour
salt
pepper

Put the dried mushrooms in a pan with 500ml/2 cups of water. Bring to the boil then cook on a low heat for 1 hour 25 minutes. Drain the liquid and keep, and chop up the mushrooms.

Put the onions in a pan with some oil and cook for 7 minutes. Add the garlic and mushroom s and cook for 20 minutes. Add some salt and pepper.

Add the flour and mix, then add the liquid from the dried mushrooms. Cook on a medium heat for 10 minutes, stirring frequently to create a thick sauce. Add the sour cream and mix.

Stewed Cabbage

Ingredients

1 sliced white cabbage
2 sliced onions
1 teaspoon of caraway seeds
half a sliced cucumber
60g/2.1 oz of tomato puree/paste
oil
parsley
salt
pepper

Put the cabbage in a bowl and sprinkle over some salt.

Fry the onion in a pan for 10 minutes.

Add the cabbage, cucumber and caraway seeds. Add
100ml/3.4 fl oz of water, cover and cook on a low heat for 25
minutes.

Add some salt and pepper and mix. Stir in the tomato puree.
cover and simmer for 30 minutes. Add some parsley before
serving.

Sauerkraut Soup

Ingredients

300g/10 oz of chopped mushrooms
160g/5.6 oz of sauerkraut
4 chopped potatoes
1 chopped carrot
1 peeled onion
1 chopped onion
5 peppercorns
2 bay leaves
fresh parsley

Put the mushrooms, bay leaf and peeled onion in a pan with 3 litres/12 cups of water. Cook on a medium heat for 25 minutes.

Drain the stock from the pan and reserve. Put the onion and mushrooms on a plate.

Put the potatoes and peppercorns in the stock in a pan and cook on a medium heat for 10 minutes -until cooked.

Put the chopped carrot and onion in a pan with some oil. Cook for 8 minutes. Put the mushrooms in the pan and cook for 6 minutes.

Put the fried onion and carrot in the pan with the potatoes and stock. Add the sauerkraut ad cook for 15 minutes on a medium heat. Add some parsley before serving.

Pyrizhky

Ingredients

dough

300ml/1 and a quarter cups of warm milk
3 tablespoons of honey
3 teaspoons of yeast
110g/3.8 oz of melted butter
2 egg yolks
sea salt
250g/8.8 oz of flour

filling

130g/4.5 oz of cooked chopped chestnuts
500g/1.1 lb of mushrooms
110g/3.8 oz of chopped onions
1 cored and chopped apple
2 chopped cloves of garlic
half a teaspoon of allspice
salt
pepper
butter
oil

To make the dough, mix the honey, yeast and milk. Leave for 8 minutes. Add the melted butter, egg yolks and a little salt.

Mix the ingredients. Add the flour and mix to make a dough. Put in a bowl, cover with plastic wrap and leave for 2 hours.

For the filling, fry the mushrooms in a pan with some butter, oil and a little salt for 10 minutes.

In another pan, fry the mushrooms in some oil and butter for 7 minutes. Add the apple, allspice and garlic to the pan and cook for 4 minutes. Add the mushrooms and some salt to the pan. Add the chestnuts and mix. Add some pepper.

Divide the dough into 10 pieces. Roll the pieces into circle shapes. Put some filling on each circle. Enclose the filling in the dough. Put on a baking tray, cover with a damp tea towel and leave for 15 minutes.

Brush the rolls with some beaten egg. Bake in a preheated oven at 180C/356F for 20 minutes.

Buckwheat with Mushrooms

Ingredients

150g/1 cup of buckwheat
400g/14 oz of chopped mushrooms
1 chopped onion
chopped fresh dill
sea salt
olive oil
500ml/2 cups of hot water
pepper

Put some olive oil in a pan and heat. Add the buckwheat and cook for 5 minutes. Add the water. Cover and cook on a low heat for 18 minutes.

Put the mushrooms, onion and some salt and pepper in a pan and cook for 15 minutes.

Serve the mushrooms with the buckwheat and top with dill.

Garlic Potatoes

Ingredients

900g/2 lb of potatoes cut into cubes
4 cloves of minced garlic
sunflower oil
fresh dill
sea salt

Put the potatoes in a pan and cover with water. Add some salt, cover and bring to the boil. Cook on a low heat for 14 minutes. Drain the potatoes.

Mix the garlic with some sunflower oil in a bowl and leave for 20 minutes.

Put the potatoes in a pan with the garlic mix, some dill and some salt. Cook for 4 minutes and stir.

Cauliflower Patties

Ingredients

1 cauliflower chopped into florets
1 beaten egg
110ml/3.7 fl oz of milk
70g/2.4 oz of buckwheat flour
salt
pepper
oil

Put the cauliflower in a bowl of boiling salted water for 5 minutes. Drain.

Mix the flour, milk, some salt and pepper and egg and make a batter.

Dip the cauliflower in the batter. Put spoonfuls of batter with about 5 cauliflower florets in them in some hot oil and cook on both sides until golden brown.

Vegetable Stew

Ingredients

half a chopped cabbage
350g/12.3 oz of chopped mushrooms
110g/3.8 oz of cooked haricot beans
1 chopped bell pepper
2 chopped carrots
2 chopped garlic cloves
black pepper
chopped fresh parsley
oil

Cook the onion, mushrooms and carrot in a pan for 17 minutes.

Add the cabbage and bell pepper and some salt to the pan with 300 ml/1 and a quarter cups of water. Cook on a low heat for 20 minutes.

Add the beans, garlic and parsley. Cook for 5 minutes.

Potato Balls

Ingredients

4 peeled and grated potatoes
250g/8.8 oz of mashed potato
125g/half a cup of farmers cheese/ricotta
fresh chopped dill
flour
1 beaten egg
dried breadcrumbs
salt
pepper

Mix the mashed and grated potatoes with some salt and pepper.

Mix the cheese and dill with some salt. Take some potato, add about a tablespoon of cheese and make a ball encasing the cheese.

Coat the balls in some flour, egg then breadcrumbs. Fry in hot oil for 12 minutes.

Fish in Wine

Ingredients

900g/2 lb of white fish fillets - for example cod - cut into
pieces
240ml/1 cup of white wine
120ml/half a cup of water
100ml/3.3 fl oz of lemon juice
1 egg yolk
butter
1 tablespoon of flour
salt
pepper

Put some salt and pepper on the fish.

Put the wine, butter and lemon juice in a saucepan. Add the
fish. Bring to to the boil then cover and cook on a low heat for
15 minutes.

Remove the fish from the pan. Mix the flour with some butter
to make a paste. Add to the liquid in the pan. Cook on a
medium heat stirring all the time for 8 minutes - until the
sauce has thickened.

Stir in the egg yolk. Add some salt and pepper and serve the
fish with the sauce.

Ukraine Christmas Facts

The Christmas bread - Kolach - is a central part of Ukrainian Christmas dinner. The three rings of the bread symbolise the Trinity and Eternity. Pieces of the bread are dipped in honey which has been blessed in church,

Uzvar is a traditional Christmas drink at the Christmas dinner. This stewed fruit drink is called God's Drink.

The Ukrainian Christmas dinner on Christmas Eve is meat free as the church in Ukraine requires fasting before Christmas day.

A traditional Ukraine Christmas dinner is twelve courses. The first course is kutia. Next is borscht with vushka - mushroom and onion dumplings. Different fish dishes are then served. Different types of varenky are served followed by stuffed cabbage - holubtsi. Uzvar rounds off the dinner.

Those who do not attend Christmas dinner with their family are thought to be lonely the next year, a Ukrainian superstition states.

Fried Trout

Ingredients

4 prepared whole trout
1 clove of chopped garlic
lemon juice
flour
fresh dill

Rub some flour on the fish. Put some oil and the garlic in a pan. Fry the fish for 5 minutes on each side in the hot oil.

Drizzle with lemon juice and garnish with dill.

Liver Cake

Baked Apple

Doughnuts

Kutia

Carp with Sour Cream

Ingredients

1.3 kg/2.8 lb of carp fillets
1 chopped onion
1 chopped carrot
butter
sunflower oil
2 tablespoons of flour
chopped fresh dill
240ml/1 cup of vegetable stock/broth
240ml/1 cup of sour cream
salt
pepper

Cook the onion in some butter in a pan for 2 minutes. Add the carrot and stock and cook on a low heat for 13 minutes.

Mix the sour cream with the flour. Put the fish in a baking dish and pour over the sour cream. Add the carrot and onion. Cover with foil. Bake in a preheated oven at 205C/400F for 20 minutes.

Ukraine Christmas Facts

Ukrainians feel it is important to forgive people who have wronged them during the year on Christmas Eve to avoid bad luck in the new year.

There is a Ukrainian story about a poor woman who could not afford to decorate a Christmas tree for her children.

At Christmas she awoke to find the tree covered in cobwebs which then turned to gold and silver when the sun came in through the window. This is called the Legend of the Christmas Spider and Ukrainians have spider ornaments on their Christmas trees.

There are two different New Year's Eve celebrations in Ukraine. One is on January 1st following the Gregorian calendar. The other is on January 14th following the Julian calendar.

Ukrainians often miss breakfast and lunch on Christmas Eve.

Fish in Aspic

Ingredients

242g/5 oz fish fillets
800ml/3 and a half cups of vegetable stock/broth
1 sliced carrot
200g/7 oz of sliced mushrooms
pepper
half a tablespoon of sugar
30g/half an oz of gelatine
1 chopped clove of garlic

Bring a pan of 500ml/2 cups water to the boil. Add the fish, cover, and cook on a low heat or 20 minutes. Put the fish on a plate.

Put 800ml/5 and a half cups of the stock in a pan. Add the sugar, garlic and some pepper. Add the carrots and mushrooms and cook for 6 minutes - until cooked. Take the vegetables out of the pan and put on a plate. Strain the stock in a bowl.

Put the gelatine in the bowl of stock and dissolve. Put 250ml/1 cup of the stock in a dish and put in the refrigerator for 40 minutes until nearly firmed up.

Cut the fish into pieces and put on top of the jelly. Put the carrots and mushrooms on top. Add the rest of the stock/gelatine mix. Put in the refrigerator for 2 hours - until set.

Trout Pie

Ingredients

2 trout fillets
4 chopped hard boiled eggs
175g/1 cup of cooked rice
200g/7 oz of sliced mushrooms
4 chopped shallots
breadcrumbs
1 beaten egg
chopped parsley
500ml/2 cups of sour cream
butter

pastry

240g/2 cups of flour
salt
5 tablespoons of butter
7 tablespoons of cold water

For the pastry, mix the ingredients together in a blender or in a bowl to make a dough. Put the dough in a bowl and leave in the refrigerator for 30 minutes.

Put the mushrooms and shallots in a pan with some butter and cook for 5 minutes.

Mix the eggs with the rice.

Mix some parsley and breadcrumbs together.

Roll out the dough. Put the breadcrumbs, trout, egg and mushroom on half the dough. Fold over the other half of the pastry to encase the filling. Cut two small slices in the top of the pastry. Brush some beaten egg on top.

Cook in a preheated oven at 204C/400F for 50 minutes.

Fish in Tomato Sauce

Ingredients

900g/2 lb of white fish fillets - for example cod
1 chopped onion
5 chopped tomatoes
100g/half a cup of chopped celery
1 chopped clove of garlic
75g/half a cup of chopped bell pepper
butter
lemon juice
flour
paprika
1 teaspoon of salt
flour
pepper

Fry the onion and celery in some butter for 6 minutes. Add the bell pepper, garlic, tomatoes and some lemon juice and pepper. cook on a low heat for 17 minutes.

Rub the mix through a sieve into a bowl. Keep the liquid.

Put some flour and salt and pepper on the fish. Fry in some butter for 6 minutes on each side.

Put the fish in a baking dish. Add the other liquid. Add some paprika. Cook on a preheated oven at 176C/350F for 25 minutes.

Shrimp with Dill

Ingredients

900g/2 lb of shelled shrimp
3 tablespoons of chopped fresh dill
2 chopped shallots
2 tablespoons of flour
250ml/1 cup of cream
2 bay leaf
240ml/1 cup of dry white wine
butter
salt
pepper

Cook the shallots in some butter for 7 minutes. Add the wine, 250ml/1 cup of water, bay leaf and shrimp. Cook on a low heat for 5 minutes. Remove from the heat.

Put some butter in a pan. Add the flour and mix with the butter to make a paste. Add the cream and cook on a medium heat, stirring all the time for 7 minutes until the sauce has thickened. Add the dill and some salt and pepper.

Put the dill sauce in the pan with the shrimp. Remove the bay leaf, then cook for 5 minutes.

Rolled Herring

Ingredients

pickled herring fillets
sliced gherkins
pickled onions
pickled mushrooms
fresh dill

Place pieces of mushroom, onion, gherkin on the herring fillets. Roll up and secure with a wooden sick.

Chicken in Jelly

Ingredients

1 chicken cut into pieces
1 carrot
1 peeled onion
100g/3.5 oz of chopped mushrooms
2 and half tablespoons of gelatin e
2 bay leaves
4 peppercorns
pepper
salt

Put the chicken in a pan and cover with cold water. Bring to the boil then cook on a low hear for 2 hours. Add the onion, peppercorns, carrot, bay leaves and some salt and pepper. Cook on a low heat for another hour.

Remove the meat from the bones, chop and place on a plate. Discard the carrot, onion, peppercorns and bay leaves.

Take 130g/4.5 oz of the chicken stock and put n a pan. Add the gelatine and cook on a medium heat for 6 minutes. Put the mix in the rest off the chicken stock.

Put the chicken into bowls or a bowl. Ad the broth and mushrooms. Put in the refrigerator for 4 hours.

Meat Patties

Ingredients

230g/half a lb of minced/ground beef
230g/half a lb of minced/ground pork
140g/5 oz of bread with no crust cut into cubes
1 finely chopped onion
1 egg
120ml/half a cup of milk
1 chopped love of garlic
1 teaspoon of salt
1 teaspoon of black pepper
nutmeg
flour
oil

Mix the bread and milk in a bowl and leave for 5 minutes. Squeeze the bread a little, then add to a bowl with the meat, garlic, salt, pepper, onion and some nutmeg. Mix well.

Put the flour in a bowl. Make small patty shapes from the meat mix. Coat in the flour. Fry in hot oil for 5 minutes on each side.

Goose With Apple

Ingredients

1 goose
800g/1.7 lb of chopped potatoes
4 chopped apples
2 chopped cloves of garlic
3 tablespoons of white wine
salt
pepper

Mix the garlic and wine with some salt and pepper. Rub the skin of the goose with the mix. Leave for 6 hours.

Put the potatoes in boiling water and cook for 6 minutes.

stuff the goose with the apple and potatoes.

Put the goose in a baking dish and cook in a preheated oven at 180C/356F for 3 hours. Baste the goose occasionally and top with foil if burning.

Ukraine Christmas Facts

On December 6th St. Nicholas Day is celebrated. The day is named after a 2nd century bishop. He delivers gifts to children on the day.

The Christmas period is considered to be mystical and allows people to find out about their future via fortune telling and divination - so the tradition goes in Ukraine.

Although the traditional number of dishes in the Ukrainian Christmas dinner is 12, some have only 7 or 9 dishes as these are superstitious numbers.

The dinner on Christmas Day - December 25th or January 7th - is called the Second Christmas Supper. Here alcohol and meat can be served.

Beef Stew

Ingredients

450g/1 lb of cubed beef pieces
4 finely chopped cloves of garlic
2 chopped onions
5 cubed potatoes
2 tablespoons of cornflour/cornstarch
500ml/2 cups of beef broth/stock
500ml/2 cups of water
220g/1 cup of tomato passata/puree
50ml/quarter of a cup of cream
4 tablespoons of chopped dill
sour cream
pepper
paprika
cumin
salt
olive oil

Cook the beef in some olive oil in a saucepan for 6 minutes. Add garlic, onion and some salt. Cook for 6 minutes. Add some pepper, cumin and paprika.

Cook for 5 minutes, then add the tomato passsata, water and beef stock. Bring to the boil then cover and cook on a low heat for 1 and a half hours.

Remove the beef and place on a plate. Add the potatoes to the pan, cover and cook on a high heat for 30 minutes -until the potatoes are cooked.

Mix the cornflour and cream. Put this mix in the pan with the beef. Stir well and cook for another 5 minutes.

Add dill and sour cream before serving.

Uzvar

Spider Christmas Tree Ornament

Liver Cake

Ingredients

450g/1 lb of chicken liver
3 grated carrots
1 chopped onion
2 cloves of garlic
130ml/half a cup of milk
2 eggs
40g/1 third of a cup of flour
340g/1 cup of mayonnaise
dill
parsley
salt
oil

Fry the onions and carrots in some oil for 8 minutes.

Blend the chicken livers with the milk to make a smooth mix.

Put the liver mix in a bowl. Add the eggs. 2 tablespoons of oil and some salt. Whisk in the flour.

From the liver batter make thin pancakes in a pan with some oil.

Mix the garlic and mayonnaise in a bowl. Add some dill and parley and some salt and pepper.

Put a pancake on a plate. spread over some mayonnaise and then some of the carrot/onion mix. Repeat for about 10 layers. Cut slices from the cake to serve.

Baked Ham

Ingredients

450g/1 lb pork fillet
1 chopped onions
15 cloves of garlic
a tablespoon of chopped mint
2 bay leaf
600ml/2 and a half cups of kvass
pepper
salt

Put the pork in a bowl. Put holes in the pork and put the garlic and onions in the them. Add some salt and pepper, the mint, bayeaf. Pour the kvass over the pork. Cover and refrigerate for 10 hours.

Put the pork on a baking tray and cook for 60 minutes in a preheated oven at 200C/392F.

Turkey Cutlet

Ingredients

800g/1.7 lb of minced/ground turkey
130g/4.5 oz of grated cheese
80g/2.8 oz of butter
40ml/1.3 fl oz of milk
breadcrumbs
thyme
chopped garlic
black pepper
salt
3 eggs
oil

Mix the turkey with the butter, eggs, milk, cheese and some salt and pepper.

Make into patties and coat in breadcrumbs. Out in the refrigerator for 40 minutes.

Put some oil in a pan with some thyme and chopped garlic and heat. Remove the thyme and garlic then fry the patties for 8 minutes on each side - until cooked.

Liver Paste

Ingredients

800g/1.7 lb of chopped chicken livers
310g/10 oz of grated carrot
410g/1 lb of finely chopped onion
150g/5.3 oz of butter
oil
pepper
salt

Fry the onion in some oil for 6 minutes.

In another pan fry the carrot in some oil for 5 minutes.

Fry the liver in a pan in some oil for 3 minutes on each side.

Put all the liver, onion and carrot in a blender and blend to make a paste.

Add the butter and some salt and pepper to the mix. Serve cooled.

Kutia

Ingredients

600g/1.3 lb of wheat berries
60g/2.11 oz of poppy seeds
110g/3.8 oz of chopped walnuts
100g/3.5 oz of raisins
4 tablespoons of honey
salt
sugar

Wash the wheat. Put 2 litres/8 cups of water a bowl and the wheat. Leave for 7 hours. Drain.

Put the wheat in a pan with 3 litres/12 cups of water. Add some salt and sugar. Boil then cover and cook on a low heat for 35 minutes. Drain the water.

Put the poppy seeds in a bowl. Cover with hot water. Leave for 1 hour. Drain the seeds then grind them- in a pestle and mortar for example - to make a paste.

Mix the nuts with the poppy seed paste. Put in a bowl. Add the wheat and raisins.

Mix 200ml/6.7 fl oz of warm water with the honey. Pour into the wheat mix.

Christmas Bread

Ingredients

6 tablespoons of raisins
6 tablespoons of dried apricot
350ml/1 and a half cups of warm milk
240g/8 oz of sugar
1 tablespoon of yeast
750g/1.6 lb of flour
80ml/2.7 fl oz of sunflower oil
110g/3.8 oz of melted butter
4 egg yolks
4 egg whites
1 teaspoon of vanilla sugar
poppy seeds
salt

Put the yeast in the milk in a bowl and dissolve. Add 150g of flour and 3 tablespoons of sugar and mix. Cover then leave for 35 minutes in a warm place.

Mix the egg yolks with the vanilla sugar, then add to the milk mix. Whisk the egg whites to make a paste then add to the bowl. Add the oil and butter and mix.

Add the rest of the flour and the raisins and apricot to the dough. Knead the dough for 10 minutes. Put the dough in a bowl, cover and leave in a warm place for 30 minutes. Roll the dough into long strips. Braid the strips together and make a circle shape with a hole in the middle. Put on a baking tray and leave for 15 minutes.

Brush with some beaten egg and sprinkle poppy seeds on top. Cook in a preheated oven at 170C/338F for 50 minutes.

Fruit and Honey Bars

Ingredients

113g/4 oz of chopped dates
113g/4 oz of chopped figs
113g/4 oz of raisins
340g/1 cup of honey
180g/1 and a half cups of flour
4 beaten eggs
baking soda/sodium bicarbonate
1 teaspoon cinnamon
salt
240ml/1 cup of vegetable oil

Mix the egg with the oil and honey. Add the flour, and a little sodium bicarbonate and salt and the cinnamon. Mix. Add the fruit and mix.

Put the mix in a greased baking tray. Cook for 53 minutes at 176C/350F. Cut into bar shapes.

Baked Apples

Ingredients

apples
chopped walnuts
poppy seeds
brown sugar
butter

Take the core out of the apples. Mix the sugar, walnuts and poppy seeds. Put the mix in the hole in the apples. Add some butter. Cook in a preheated oven at 200C/392F for 30 minutes.

Nougat

Ingredients

400g/2 cups of sugar
110g/1 third of a cup of golden syrup/corn syrup
240ml/1 cup of water
4 whipped egg whites
1 teaspoon of vanilla
200g/7 oz of chopped nuts
70g/half a cup of glace/candied cherries

Put the water, corn syrup and sugar in a pan. Boil on a
medium heat for 15 minutes - until stiffened.

Remove from the heat and mix the egg whites with the syrup
mix and blend for 5 minutes.

Add the rest of the ingredients, then pour into greased baking
dishes. Leave for 10 hours then cut into pieces.

Cheesecake

Ingredients

280g/10 oz of cherries with stone taken out
120g/4.2 oz of raisins
800g/1.7 lb of farmers/ricotta cheese
130g/4.6 oz of butter
600g/1.3 lb of caster sugar
4 eggs
350g/12.5 oz of flour
melted butter
1 teaspoon of baking powder
vanilla extract
110ml/half a cup of lemon juice
salt

Mix the butter, 80g/2.8 oz of sugar and a little salt together. Add 1 beaten egg and mix. Add 300g/10 oz of the flour and baking powder. Mix. Grease a pan, then press the mix to the side to make pastry case. Place in the refrigerator for 40 minutes.

Put the raisins in some hot water and leave for 6 minutes. Drain.

Put the cheese in a sieve and push into a bowl. Add some lemon zest, 50g/1.7 oz of flour and some vanilla extract to the cheese. Whisk together. Add 3 beaten eggs and whisk well for 7 minutes, Add 340g/12 oz of sugar, some melted butter and the raisins and mix well.

Put 180g/6.3 oz of caster sugar, lemon juice and 240ml/1 cup of water in a pan. Cook on a medium heat for 12 minutes stirring frequently. Add the cheeses, boil then cook for 12 minutes.

Put the cherries on a plate and cook the syrup for another 9 minutes. Mix the cherries with the syrup.

Put the pastry in a preheated oven at 190C/374F and cook for 15 minutes.

Put the cheese mix into the pastry case. Cook in a preheated oven at 150C/302F for 1 hour. Refrigerate for 5 hours. Add some of cherry sauce before serving.

Snowball Cookies

Ingredients

75g/half cup of chopped nuts
226g/1 cup of butter
230/half cup of icing/confectioners' sugar
260g/9 oz of flour
vanilla extract
salt

Mix the sugar, butter and some salt in a bowl. Add some vanilla extract and mix. Mix in the flour. Add the nuts and mix.

Place the dough in the refrigerator for 5 hours.

Form small balls from the dough. Place on a baking sheet and cook in a preheated oven at 204C/400F for 13 minutes. Coat in powdered sugar.

Sour Cream Cake

Ingredients

240g/2 cups of flour
7 eggs
200g/1 cup sugar
340g/1 cup of honey
2 teaspoons of baking soda
salt
1 tablespoon of lemon juice
400ml/14 fl oz of sour cream

frosting

200g/7 oz cream cheese
141g/5 oz cream
45g/half cup of icing/confectioners' sugar

Mix the eggs, sugar and a little salt for 8 minutes to make a smooth paste.

Mix the baking soda and lemon juice. Mix with the honey and sour cream. Add to the egg mix. Whisk the flour into the batter.

Put the batter into a baking dish. Cook for 30 minutes in a preheated oven at 176C/350F. Cool then cut into squares.

Mix the frosting ingredients to make a paste. Pipe onto the cakes.

Vanilla Cookies

Ingredients

85g/3 oz ground almonds
226g/8 oz of butter
100g/half a cup of sugar
1 tablespoon of vanilla extract
240g/2 cups of flour
half a teaspoon of baking powder
2 tablespoons of milk
1 tablespoon of confectioners sugar
1 tablespoon of vanilla sugar

Mix the butter and sugar to make a paste. Add the vanilla extract and almonds.

Mix the flour and baking powder. Add to the butter mix with the milk and make a dough.

Grease a baking tray. Make small balls from the dough, then form into crescent shapes. Place on the baking tray and cook in a preheated oven at 176C/350F for 10 minutes.

Mix the vanilla sugar and confectioners sugar and dust the cookies with the mix.

Honey Cake

Ingredients

240g/1 cup of honey
2 teaspoons of cinnamon
300g/2 cups of raisins
150g/2 cups of chopped walnuts
360g/3 cups of flour
1 teaspoon of baking powder
salt
240g/8 oz of butter
3 teaspoons of baking powder
4 egg yolks
4 egg whites
215g/1 cup of brown sugar
4 tablespoons of liquid coffee

Mix the honey and cinnamon in a pan. Boil, then cool. Mix the raisins and walnuts with 3 tablespoons of flour.

Mix the baking soda, salt and rest of the flour.

Mix the butter and sugar to make a paste. Mix in the egg yolks. Add the honey mix, flour mix and coffee. Stir then add the walnut and raisin mix.

Whisk the egg whites until stiff then add to the other mix.

Grease a baking dish then pour in the mix. Cook in a preheated oven at 162C/325F for 75 minutes.

Doughnuts

Ingredients

2 eggs
240ml/1 cup of warm milk
2 tablespoons of melted butter
2 tablespoons of sugar
salt
1 teaspoon of vanilla extract
1 teaspoon of yeast
240g/2 cups of flour
icing/powdered sugar
oil
strawberry jam

Put the yeast in a little warm milk and leave for 10 minutes.

Mix the milk, yeast with milk eggs, sugar, butter, vanilla extract and some salt in a bowl. Mix in the flour to make a dough.

Knead the dough for 5 minutes. Roll the dough into a ball, place in an oiled bowl, cover with plastic wrap and leave for 2 hours.

Roll out the dough. Cut into round cookie sized shapes. Put on a greased baking sheet and leave for 30 minutes.

Fry the doughnuts in hot oil until brown on both sides.

Leave to cool, then pipe strawberry jam into them using a piping bag. Coat the doughnuts in some powdered sugar.

Scuffles

Ingredients

360g/3 cups of flour
1 tablespoon of yeast
5 tablespoons of warm water
salt
3 tablespoons of sugar
226g/1 cup of butter
120ml/half a cup of milk
2 beaten eggs
200g/1 cup of sugar
1 and a half tablespoons of cinnamon

Put the yeast in the water and leave for 10 minutes.

Mix the flour, 3 tablespoons of sugar, butter and some salt in a bowl. Add the milk, eggs and yeast. Make a dough. Knead the dough for 5 minutes. Put the dough in a greased bowl, cover with plastic wrap and place in the refrigerator for 10 hours.

Mix the 3 cups of sugar with the cinnamon. Cut the dough into six. Roll out the dough pieces on the sugar/cinnamon mix. Create a round shape from each dough piece and cut into wedge shapes. Roll the wedges up starting at the pointed end. Place on a greased baking sheet and cook in a preheated oven at 176C/350F for 20 minutes.

Cherry Kisel

Ingredients

800g/2 lb of cherries
water
200g/1 cup of sugar
salt
6 tablespoons of potato flour/potato starch

Put 3 litres/12 cups of water in a pan and bring to the boil. Add the cherries. Boil then cook on a low heat for 12 minutes. Add the sugar, stir for 5 minutes then cook on a low heat for another 5 minutes.

Drain the liquid into a bowl using a strainer. Add 100ml/3.3 fl oz of water and the potato flour to the liquid and stir. Put in a pan with a little salt and bring to the boil stirring all the time. Cook on a low heat for 5 minutes.

Can be drank hot or cold.

Uzvar

Ingredients

141g/5 oz of dried prunes - with stone taken out
141g/5 oz of raisins
226g/8 oz of dried pear slices
255g/9 oz of sliced dried apple
340g/1 cup of honey
7 cloves
1 stick of cinnamon
2 litres/8 cups of water

Put the ingredients, apart from the honey in a pan. Cook on a low heat for 30 minutes

Add the honey and bring to the boil.

Strain and serve hot or cold in glasses. The fruit can be served separately.

2013
UKRAINA
УКРАЇНА
2.50

www.ingramcontent.com/pod-product-compliance
Lightning Source LLC
Chambersburg PA
CBHW021130130726
47988CB00003B/1238